The Restaurant Resource Series:

A Beginners Guide to Restaurant and Bar Start-ups

Gregrey Michael Carpenter

Defining the Restaurant Concept

The restaurant concept or theme is basically the image you need to convey to your public. But before you even begin the procedure you must decide regarding the concept. Throughout the early stages, a few of the specifics regarding the restaurant concept is supposed to be tentative. However, when you have identified a potential location and worked through a few of the operational and financial issues, you might need in order to make modification to your concept. Nevertheless, it's still required to develop a working idea associated with the restaurant concept to enable you to begin determining the requirements for starting the operation.

Many for the decisions that has to be made when starting a restaurant is supposed to be driven by the initial decision about the restaurant's concept. Defining the idea includes determining the operations:

1.Menu

2. Atmosphere

3. Prices

4. Target customers

The Menu

Even though the concept is more than simply the food served to the majority of observers, the menu is the shortcut way to describe the idea. It certainly is the most essential element to consider when developing a potential restaurant's concept.

During the early stages, it is really not required to determine a precise menu or recipes, however, a basic idea of this menu is necessary to ensure the restaurateur can evaluate the following:

1. Potential competitors. The wide range of restaurants offering similar menus is supposed to be an important aspect of selecting a place.

2. Sources of supply. This really is especially important in the event that proposed menu requires special or difficult to find ingredients.

3. Equipment or layout requirements. Kitchen equipment needs will vary dependent on the idea. For instance, the equipment needed to serve Mexican food differs substantially through the requirements of a steakhouse.

4. Special personnel skills. Some menu items needs to be prepared by specially skilled kitchen personnel.

The Atmosphere

A restaurant's atmosphere, such as formal or casual, is another important element associated with overall concept that has to be considered when making start-up decisions. A few of the issues pertaining to atmosphere include:

1. Design elements. Typically, atmosphere is reflected throughout a restaurant by its china, servers, furnishings, glassware' uniforms, and menu style. Accordingly, the atmosphere may dictate the type and expense of various items.

2. Special personnel skills. In a few cases, the atmosphere may dictate that employees with special skills needs to be

hired. For instance, you might need special servers to serve some items which require table side preparation.

In most cases, the specific decisions relating to restaurant atmosphere, such as furniture or china purchases, can be deferred until following the site is selected. However, the intended design of this operation could have a bearing when considering the suitability of a potential site, which we are going to discuss later.

Prices

A restaurant's price structure is affected by its menu as well as its atmosphere. Generally, however, specific costs are not considered until the restaurant has established the last menu.

Target Customers

A restaurant's choices in menu, atmosphere, and costs are generally made using the objective of attracting a particular kind of customer, such as young families, young professionals, or elderly people.

Other factors associated with concept include:

Level of service.

a. Full table service restaurants, in which servers are employed to take and deliver orders.

b. No table service restaurants, that do not employ servers. In these establishments customers place and pick up their particular orders, and often bus their own tables.

The planned level of service will affect the decisions built in starting a restaurant within the following area.

a. Restaurant layout. When selecting a website, the level of service will affect the way the restaurant is configured.

b. Staffing levels. The level of service will affect the type and wide range of employees hired.

Menu Range

In most cases, a restaurant offering a full range of menu items will demand a much larger kitchen area to prepare all regarding the items. It is important to determine in the event that kitchen and storeroom areas are adequate for the planned menu range.

Determining a Location

The most important steps in starting a restaurant is selecting a proper location. Determining a place is more than simply signing a lease. Extensive search needs to be done to determine your potential employees, customers and your competitors. What considerations if you be shopping for in a website? I believe the four to be:

1. Customer base

2. Competition

3. Personnel availability

4. Site characteristics

Customer Base

The area in which a restaurant can draw its customers will vary greatly. Many people will travel a good distance to consume at a restaurant that is a local institution, whereas a lunch operation in an office building may only draw customers from an area no bigger than a city block. When evaluating the client base, even though it is important to understand the total number of individuals in an area, it is even more important to determine the number of potential customers.

Temporary Population

Potential customers include both full-time residents and also the temporary population. The temporary population is consists of individuals who live elsewhere and visit, or work, into the area. This might be often an important supply of restaurant customers. However, it is important to note the supply of the temporary population. Office workers, instead of factory workers are typically a better supply of customers. Seek the advice of the local chamber of commerce; most likely they may be able provide you with data to aid you quantify the dimensions and nature of temporary populations.

The greater that is known about the potential customers, the better chance there is of establishing a restaurant that will appeal to a bigger audience. This might be often carried out by analyzing census along with other data available on the internet or through the local chambers of commerce. Observation of this traffic patterns at other restaurants into the area will help in identifying potential customers.

Restaurant Statistics

Each restaurant, year business magazines publish statistics that indicate the potential of restaurants in various major metropolitan areas. The two statistical measures are the restaurant activity index additionally the restaurant growth index.

a. Restaurant Activity Index (RAI). This measures the tendency for the population into the area to consume out. An RAI of 100 means that the willingness for eating out is the identical because the national average. An RAI of less than 100 indicates a less than average tendency to consume out.

b. Restaurant Growth Index (RGI). This measures the relationship of restaurant supply and demand. An RGI of 100 indicates an adequate wide range of restaurants relative to demand. An RGI of less than 100 is a situation where supply exceeds demand. Conversely, an RGI greater than 100 indicates that the area could support additional restaurants.

One major problem with these statistics is the fact that they encompass entire metropolitan areas. They're not particularly useful when attempting to determine a particular neighborhood location. Therefore, it can be required to conduct some informal research to gauge the potential of a new restaurant in a particular area.

The most effective techniques to evaluate the possibility of a new restaurant site is to consider the competition. Since it is unlikely that existing managers or owners will talk about their operation to a potential competitor, you must accomplish this task by observation. This involves:

a. Identifying all of the restaurants into the immediate area and estimating the total wide range of seats.

b. Identifying the "like competitors" (i.e., those restaurants identified in "a.") which have an identical menu prices, concepts, or target audiences.

c. Narrowing the like competitors right down to five restaurants which are considered to be direct competition. This might be certainly usually done according to one or higher associated with the following factors:

Reputation

Similarity of concepts

Similarity of menu prices

Proximity to your proposed location.

Additionally, you will have to document the following information for each direct competitor you identify:

a. Concept

b. If liquor is sold

c. Menu price range

d. Distance from proposed location

e. Visibility compared to proposed location

f. Accessibility compared to proposed location

g. Hours

h. Observed percentage of capacity at: 1) Breakfast, 2) Lunch and 3) Dinner

Generally, the absolute most effective way to obtain this info is by going to each one of the identified competitors.

Personnel Availability

An owner considering additional or new operation should ensure there is a sufficient wide range of willing workers available. In a lot of locations, it is not a major consideration since there is going to be many those who are willing to operate in restaurants. However, in a few areas of the nation, restaurant workers have been in very short supply.

Site Characteristics

When you have determined that the area you have selected has enough potential customers to achieve success, the very first step is to evaluate the proposed site. Site selection may not be overemphasized. Countless restaurants have failed because of unsuitable locations. Two of the most extremely important aspects of selecting a website are:

a. Visibility. In short, having the ability to begin to see the restaurant will motivate many potential customers to test it. This really is especially important when starting a new operation. A restaurant based in an out-of-the-way location loses a ready supply of free advertising in its visibility to pedestrians and motorists passing by.

b. Accessibility. Although visibility is an important aspect of developing public desire for a restaurant, its accessibility will most likely determine in the event that customer actually dines there. Although customers could possibly see a restaurant, they might not really you will need to get there if access appears difficult.

Visibility and accessibility are usually considered together. The following are some things to consider when evaluating a potential site's visibility and accessibility.

a. Convenience. This might be actually the measure of this site's proximity to potential customers. Many of these sources

include:

1. Residential areas.

2. Shopping centers.

3. Educational facilities.

4. Recreational areas.

5. Central business district.

6. Industrial centers.

7. Mass transportation stops.

8. Freeway exits.

b. Traffic Count. This might be certainly primarily a measure of visibility that involves measuring the wide range of pedestrians and cars that pass by the website. The speed of passing cars should additionally be considered. Unless the restaurant is visible for some cars, distance driving by at speeds greater than 35 to 40 miles per hour might not be able to react in time for you actually stop during the restaurant (even though this can be overcome by having easy access and strategic placement of advertisements).

In addition to location, the physical design (physical attributes) regarding the site should additionally be evaluated. This consists of:

a. Physical suitability. The physical layout of this site needs to be suitable for the envisioned restaurant concept. If another unit of an existing concept is being opened, it is preferable to have the latest unit the same size and configuration due to the fact other units. This can help lower the expenses of finishing out of the space, since many associated with design decisions and specifications can be carried over from previous experience.

b. Parking facilities. Adequate parking facilities are an important consideration for nearly all restaurants. If you do not are locating a restaurant downtown, adequate parking ought to be available for both employees and customers.

c. Adequacy of utilities. The capacity to obtain electric, gas, water, and waste disposal services is also essential.

d. Municipal services. The adequacy of police and fire protection, as well as sanitation services, needs to be considered. These services have an impact on the restaurant's ability to attract employees and customers and may affect the restaurant's insurance rates.

e. Zoning considerations. Although appropriate zoning is a concern for almost any restaurants, business may face additional requirements. This might be certainly especially true in the event that restaurant intends to serve liquor.

Once a website for a new restaurant happens to be selected, the restaurateur must determine just how to secure its use. For most new restaurants, this will entail the negotiation and execution of a lease. A commercial real estate lease will probably end up being the single largest legal and financial commitment that a restaurant will have. Since restaurateurs do not usually have the the bargaining or knowledge leverage required to ensure that the greatest possible lease terms are obtained, they usually need good legal and business advice.

The following are a few of the more important features of a lease agreement:

a. Term. The duration of the lease ought to be consistent with all the plans and objectives regarding the new restaurant.

b. Flexibility. The following questions can be asked to see whether the lease offers the restaurateur with all the necessary flexibility.

1. Exactly what are the renewal provisions?

2. If additional space is not available when needed, and relocation is necessary, can the tenant sublease?

3. If subleasing is allowed, are there any restrictions?

c. Cost. A gross lease excludes taxes, insurance, and repairs while a net lease passes some or a few of these expenses to a tenant. If escalation clauses are incorporated into the contract, the lessee should have a thorough comprehension of how increases are calculated. It should additionally be clear who pays for improvements and what aspects regarding the cost are negotiable.

d. Tenant common expenses. When space is rented in locations where common areas are shared along with other tenants, such as in shopping centers and malls, each tenant is normally accountable for a part of common expenses. These costs can be significant and really should be carefully considered.

e. Exposures. Two major exposures that usually can be mitigated to some degree are (1) the possibility of bankruptcy or insolvency in the an element of the landlord and (2) the possibility of rental to undesirable tenants during the same location. Financial condition of this landlord generally can be verified and then a relatively narrow limit on undesirable tenants (e.g., competitors or unsavory businesses) can be negotiated.

The high failure rate experienced by new restaurants means that, in most areas of the nation, there are usually a wide range of vacant restaurants available for lease. Many failed restaurant locations are reopened by new owners who think they may be able succeed along with their own concept. However, all too often, the latest operator fails because the negatives for the location can't be overcome. Available locations, often fully equipped, presents a chance to your careful operator. The following are a few of the advantages and disadvantages of converting a vacant restaurant into a new one.

Advantages:

• Rent concessions.

In a lot of landlords, cases are willing to offer attractive rates to some other restaurant to occupy the empty space.

• Fixtures and equipment.

Often, the proposed site includes a fully equipped kitchen as well because the fixtures within the dining area. During the very least, the website will often have a useable floor plan in position for food preparation and serving. This might be often beneficial because the less work that a new operator has to do in order to prepare the website, the lower the start-up costs will likely be.

• Reducing potential competition.

The probability of rent concessions while the accessibility to an equipped site may lure potential competitors who might not otherwise have the financial resources to start a restaurant. Therefore, leasing a former restaurant site may improve a restaurateur's changes of success by keeping out one more competitor.

Disadvantages:

• Suspect location.

The reason why the restaurant site is available can be that the location was so suspect as well as its chances of success were crippled from the beginning. Occupying such a website ought to be done with great caution. The owner deciding to do so should develop a plan of action for overcoming the location problems. Some tactics might include marketing, more visible signs, valet parking, and increased security. A full demographic study ought to be completed before signing the lease. It's been my experience that visibility and access plays a crucial role into the chances of success for almost any restaurant.

• Public memory.

Some restaurants fail because the the service or food is especially bad. In a few extreme incidents, cases of food poisoning or health code violations could have caused the operation's failure. The general public tends to remember such incidents and may even regard any successor operation with suspicion. A poor public perception can be very difficult, if you don't impossible to conquer. To be able to improve public perception you can expect to be needed to allocate a substantial amount of funds toward local store marketing.

- Design difficulties.

Sometimes a restaurant fails due to flaws within the restaurant's design; causing more than necessary labor costs to serve and cook meals. A restaurant looking to convert an existing site ought to be careful never to inherit someone else's problems. Also, a restaurant design that is suitable for one concept might not be suitable for the next. For instance, the preparation areas of an oriental restaurant will have a substantially different layout compared to those of a steak house. Therefore, it is important that a restaurateur consider the way the existing layout can be adapted to your planned concept. I would personally recommend calling in a design consultant to analyze what layout changes would be necessary.

Restaurant Fixtures and Equipment

Whether an existing restaurant is purchased, or a new operation takes over a previously occupied space, some or all of this fixtures and equipment can be offered for sale to your new owner. No matter what the concept, many for the fixtures and equipment found in a typical restaurant are typical to all restaurants. For instance, some concepts might need that a particular type of furniture be used or that the kitchen include certain specialized equipment. However the requirement for much associated with the higher cost kitchen equipment, such as refrigerators, freezers, and stoves, is common to virtually all restaurants. Ordinarily, the latest operator should evaluate the suitability associated with equipment and fixtures by:

a. Obtaining (or compiling) a total set of the available equipment and furniture.

b. Noting the condition and age of each item.

c. Identifying any equipment that is unsuitable or unusable for the latest operation.

d. Determining if any regarding the equipment and fixtures is leased.

Starting a new restaurant is not cheap. In fact, the price of building and outfitting free-standing, full service restaurant can easily exceed $1.50 million (not including land costs).

Converting an existing restaurant site, therefore, can lead to large savings. However, you need to approach any conversion with caution. There are factors why restaurants fail, and understanding those reasons is critical. Using this in your mind, taking on a former restaurant site might not be a great bargain in the event that costs of overcoming the flaws are way too high.

Operating Considerations

There are literally dozens of steps that has to be completed after making a choice on the restaurant concept and determining where to locate it, prior to it being ready to start. These considerations are divided into the following categories:

a. Administrative matters.

b. Control and accounting systems.

c. Promotion and marketing.

d. Purchasing and inventory.

e. Hiring personnel.

f. Fixed asset acquisition.

Adopting an Operating Plan…

The time through the original decision to start a restaurant to your actual opening can stretch for a lot of months. Failure to consider one step early enough within the process could impact the prosperity of the opening. For instance, in a few cases, a liquor license may simply be obtained after negotiations utilizing the local municipality which can last for several months.

In the event that application is not started in time, the operations might not have a liquor license in position by opening day. Accordingly, it is imperative that the restaurateur adopt a plan that includes a timetable to make sure that the operation's opening is successful.

Administrative Matters.

Like most start-up business, a new restaurant must address a variety of administrative matters. A few of the more important issues include:

a. Restaurant name.

b. As a type of entity.

c. Permits and licenses.

d. Insurance coverage.

The restaurant name. In most cases, the restaurant name is determined as soon as the restaurateur decides in the restaurant concept. However, before ordering menus, the owner and signs should register the name and determine that no other entity has the rights to that name. A restaurant that inadvertently uses a name which has been reserved by another entity could need to incur the expense of changing menus, signs, and every other feature within the restaurant that carried that name. Also, any marketing efforts that focused on building name recognition for the restaurant would be wasted in the event that name is changed. Trade names are generally registered utilizing the state agency that handles incorporations. In most cases, a lawyer ought to be consulted to register the name.

As a type of entity. The owner will also need to consider the advantages and disadvantages of this various types of entity which can be chosen. Restaurants typically choose among the following types of entity:

a. Proprietorship

b. General partnership

c. Limited partnership

d. Corporation (either S corporation or C corporation)

When the as a type of entity is decided, the restaurant can apply for the identification numbers, including the Employers Identification Number (EIN) through the Internal Revenue Service. The restaurant must also obtain certain licenses and permits which are unique for their operations including:

a. Health permit

b. Liquor license

c. Music copyright license.

The requirements for health permits vary substantially between jurisdictions, with a few areas being stricter than the others. Virtually all health permits are granted only following the restaurant passes a health inspection. Therefore, it is important to understand the local requirements at the beginning of the procedure to make sure that any planned dining or kitchen room configuration will likely to be according to the local health department rules. The local restaurant association can often provide information about required permits and licenses.

A word about music copyrights. In the event that restaurant intends to play recorded or live music (including music played on a iPod), it should obtain a copyright license through the appropriate music licensing agency. The two primary agencies are the American Society of Composers, Authors & Publishers (ASCAP) and Broadcast Music, Inc. (BMI).

Insurance Coverage. Restaurants typically have a significant amount invested in their facilities. Accordingly, the restaurateur should arrange for appropriate insurance coverage. A few of the common coverage includes:

a. Liquor liability.

b. General liability.

c. Worker's compensation.

d. Fire.

e. Business interruption.

f. Burglary.

g. Glass breakage.

h. Contents.

i. Sprinkler damage.

j. Key person.

k. Fidelity.

l. Employee benefits (life, disability, health).

This step is normally accomplished by consulting with all the restaurant's insurance agent.

Accounting and Control Systems

A restaurateur can expect to incur substantial costs as an element of preparing a restaurant for opening. Accordingly, it is important to determine accounting and control system at the beginning of the procedure to make sure that expenses are properly tracked. Establishing a free account system includes the following steps:

a) Adopt a chart of accounts and general ledger.

b) Establish banking relationships and cash handling procedures.

c) Designate persons accountable for cashier function.

d) Adopt a weekly profit and loss report along with other forms.

e) Assign responsibility for preparation of reports.

Adopt a Chart of Accounts and General Ledger. What needs to be decided is whether or perhaps not the restaurant will employ a bookkeeper to retain the ledger and accounting records. I prefer to create up everything on Quickbooks.

Establish Banking Relationships and Cash Handling Procedures. Although the restaurant is preparing for opening, it's going to be required to pay contractors along with other parties, such as employees and suppliers active in the remodeling. Therefore, most restaurateurs will establish a banking relationship at the beginning of the start-up process.

Designate Persons Accountable For Cashier Function. It's going to be required to make sure cash disbursements due to the fact start-up phase progresses. In a lot of cases, the owner personally writes those checks. In other cases, particularly if the owner is not always present, he or she may delegate the authority to pay start-up expenses. Even though the restaurant has not opened, the restaurant should determine the way the cashier function are going to be handled. A restaurant can have a central cashier or have a server that will act as a cashier. That decision may affect the restaurant's layout and personnel hiring decisions.

Adopt Weekly Profit and Loss Report along with other Forms. Even though it is not strictly required to adopt a weekly profit and loss format until the restaurant is able to open, a restaurateur should have a sense of the style of information which he or she wants from such a form prior to the point of sale system is ordered.

Assign Responsibility for Preparation of Reports. Although preparation associated with weekly profit and loss report (as well as its related forms) will not occur until following the restaurant has opened, the owner should decide who can be accountable for preparing the different reports prior to opening. By assigning this responsibility early, the owner is able to determine the work flow for information, and discover if the restaurant's information needs will impact the level of staff needed or the kind of point of sales system to install.

Marketing and Promotion

Some strategies that you might wish to consider is the opening of a new restaurant include:

a. Print Advertising.

b. TV and Radio advertising.

c. Direct mail.

d. Neighborhood fliers.

e. Coupon programs.

f. Public relations.

g. Special banners and signs in the restaurant.

h. Special promotions or meals.

i. Pre-opening meals served for selected parties (such as charitable groups or reporters).

j. Social Media

The level of promotion which will be required to publicize a newly-opened restaurant will depend, to a large extent, regarding the restaurant's location as well as its reputation. A restaurant that is located on a corner during the intersection of two busy streets may only have to place a "Now Open" banner regarding the building to attract customers. Similarly, a well established restaurant that is opening at another location will not require to operate as hard at name recognition, since the operation's name is familiar using the dinning public. A restaurant which is not well known or well located will need to develop marketing and budget intend to alert the general public to the fact that the restaurant happens to be open.

When the site happens to be determined, the restaurateur should evaluate the menu and discover its influence on purchasing and inventory requirements. This usually requires which you:

a. Finalized the menu.

b. Establish a recipe file.

c. Price the menu.

d. Place initial beverage and food orders.

Finalize the menu. Typically, when determining the restaurant concept, the preliminary menu is confined to your entrees that the proposed operation intends to serve. For instance, a steak house concept might formulate a preliminary menu according to the kinds of steaks to be served additionally the planned cooking method. While the restaurant prepares for opening, it is important to round out of the preliminary menu by making a choice on the specifics of this menu, including:

a) Appetizers

b) Salads

c) Entrees

d) Desserts

e) Non-alcoholic beverages

f) Beer, wine, and liquor selections

When the menu is finalized, the restaurateur can develop the recipes which will be useful for each item.

Establish a Recipe File. A recipe file is a significant part of establishing portion standards. While you prepare for the opening, the most important tasks is to develop recipes for each menu item. Generally, there are a variety of different techniques to prepare a menu item. The chef often goes through a procedure of testing and refining recipes until he or she settles in the recipe which will be incorporated into the file. Obviously, the main objective of this testing phase is to develop a recipe that will taste good to your public. However, there are two main other important objectives.

a) Develop preparation standards. A recipe will never be suitable if it may not be prepared efficiently into the kitchen. Therefore, for that reason the chef should set standards for the period of time needed to prepare the entrée. For instance, a restaurant might set a standard of 4 minutes to prepare a lunch item and 12 minutes to prepare a dinner item. By setting a preparation standard, the chef can identify overly complex recipes that need simplification. In the event that revised item cannot meet the preparation standard, it ought to be dropped through the menu.

b) Develop portion standards. When the recipe if finalized, portion standards can be developed. Setting standard portions allows you to accurately price the determine and menu initial inventory needs.

The bar manager should also develop a recipe file for all alcohol based drinks incorporated into the bar menu.

Purchasing and Inventory

The entire process of pricing the menu is no different for a start-up restaurant compared to a well established operation. The restaurateur determines the portion price of each item, and calculates the menu price using among the approved methods for menu pricing. Unlike a proven restaurant, a start-up operator will do not have direct knowledge regarding the target customers' price resistance, and runs a threat of setting its menu prices too high. In such a situation, the initial patrons might not come back, and additionally, they might complain about the costs for their friends. However, in the event that start-up restaurant's menu costs are in line utilizing the prices of near-by restaurants, price resistance is generally not a major problem.

When you have established the costs, the menus can be ordered. Based on the style printing, selected a menu can take up to two months. Accordingly, you need to take printing time into consideration to make certain your menus are ready for opening day.

In most start-up situation you should look at the amount of inventory needed for pre-opening testing. The preopening testing phase allows the kitchen staff additionally the servers to the office together in delivering, preparing and ordering actual meals. It is a significant part of preparing a restaurant for opening because this phase often identifies bottlenecks or rough spots within the operation that need fixing or fine tuning before opening day.

Pre-opening testing can additionally be made an element of the marketing and promotion program by inviting parties, such as newspaper reporters or charitable organizations, to your restaurant. However, in the event that public is served as an element of the preopening phase, all business and health permits ought to be to be able.

Make sure you complete a physical inventory of all of the food and beverage inventories regarding the night prior to the restaurant opens. Doing so provides a starting point that enables you to track food costs accurately from day one.

Hiring Personnel

Even though the basic considerations for hiring restaurant employees in a start-up situation are exactly the same as for established operations, the job is complicated by the fact that an entire staff needs to be hires at once. The steps which are typically followed when initially hiring personnel include:

a. Identify required staffing levels.

b. Develop procedures to make sure that:

   • Job application process is according to the ADA

   • Forms I-9 are obtained for all employees.

c. Develop job descriptions for all employees.

d. Develop a job application form.

e. Develop personnel policies and adopt a pay scale for all positions.

f. Place ads and signs to inform potential employees that the restaurant is hiring.

g. Interview and select employees.

h. Schedule training and orientation sessions before opening date.

i. Prepare the schedule for opening week.

Required Staffing Levels

Staffing levels can be efficiently determined making use of the Labor Staffing Chart, which provides a pictorial representation regarding the restaurant's personnel needs. One difficulty facing a manager completing this form for a start-up operation is the fact that he or she will need to guess as to which days or periods will likely to be slow or busy. Accordingly, the initial decision about staffing levels ought to be monitored and corrected, if required, following the restaurant opens.

Its also wise to consider the necessity to employ a few employees to aid with setting up the restaurant. One or two employees hired two to four weeks prior to opening can often be useful in performing tasks such as:

a. Setting up the store room and bar area.

b. Testing and cleaning equipment.

c. Storing glassware, silverware, china, and linen.

Training and Orientation

In a well established restaurant, a new employee can be quickly trained and oriented by pairing him or her up with an experienced employee who is able to show the brand new employee the restaurant's procedures. In a start-up situation, having said that, it is important to initially train all employees prior to the restaurant opens. A few of the difficulty into the initial training phase can be overcome in hiring employees with previous restaurant experience. Employees with prior experience understand their basic job, (i.e., cook, server, etc.) and need only be taught the special procedures or equipment that makes your restaurant unique.

When I noted earlier, many restaurants conduct a pre-opening testing phase in that the kitchen and servers staff practice processing meals, as well as working together with one another. This might be a tremendously efficient option to work any kinks out from the restaurant's system. Although, if it goes too long, it can turn out to be very expensive, since the employees are earning wages while no revenues are being generated. an option to control the expense of pre-opening testing to limit it to a few evenings or days before opening. Another method is to designate a core number of employees who can be in the payroll for pre-opening training. These core employees would be accountable for training the other employees when the restaurant opens.

As a practical matter, most patrons allow a new establishment a few weeks to refine their procedures. Therefore, even though it would be nice to have the employees performing flawlessly on opening day, it probably will not happen. You need to attempt to strike a balance that delivers as much training as financially possible.

Opening Week Schedule

Among the ingredients to your success of a new restaurant is adequate scheduling of staff. However, it is really not always possible to predict opening demand with certainty. Therefore, many operators elect to schedule their opening week staff levels in the heavy side to make sure that there may be enough individuals to adequately serve customers. That is probably necessary in the event that restaurant only trained a core group of employees into the pre-opening testing phase. In such a case, the other employees can be training throughout the opening week. One major pitfall to scheduling a lot of employees is the fact that it can hamper your operation. You must search for balance.

Financial Considerations

The expense of starting a restaurant, coupled because of the high failure rate associated with new restaurants, dictates a tremendously careful evaluation associated with financial aspects of any restaurant start-up or acquisition. Banks along with other lenders are traditionally very cautious about lending money to beginning restaurateurs. Consequently, the owner's capital, as well as compared to his or her family or friends is frequently at risk. In the event that restaurant is not properly capitalized right from the start it might probably fail since it is often not possible to obtain loans to tide it over until the operation gets established.

to anyone considering starting a restaurant is to complete the following:

a. Carefully evaluate the financial feasibility of the restaurant

b. Project your total capital needs

c. Project your operating results

d. Assess operating results

e. Determine worst case scenario.

d. Get the proper assistance through the experts

Starting a new restaurant venture is an enormous undertaking. Please feel free to contact Greg Carpenter at 714-986-4898 if you have any questions, or if we can provide additional assistance.

Printed in Great Britain
by Amazon.co.uk, Ltd.,
Marston Gate.